The Bashful Man –
The Story of Henry Hunnings

Clergyman and Inventor

Alan Swain

ISBN 978-1-904446-91-0

Published and printed by
Quacks Books
7 Grape Lane
Petergate
York YO1 7HU

Contents

Introduction

Henry Hunnings was a relatively unknown high-achiever from the late 1800s who has been largely overlooked in history and generally not a great deal is known about him. What has been written about him has mostly focused on his invention – the carbon-granule telephone transmitter - which was widely used around the world for a hundred years or so until it was replaced in the 1980s.

The story of his life, with its twists and turns, is representative of the life and times of post industrial revolution Victorian Britain. It tells the story of an ordinary young man from Tottenham who, like many others, left school and joined the family business. However, Henry Hunnings dreamed of greater things, he wanted to do something and be someone and was well on the way to fulfilling these ambitions by the time he reached the age of 37. But then things changed and life didn't quite work out how he would have wished.

My curiosity with Hunnings is two-fold: Firstly from my knowledge of the telephone as I worked for British Telecom for many years beginning in the days when it was the General Post Office (GPO); secondly from my love of the beautiful church that graces the village of Bolton Percy near York. Hunnings was someone who bridged both of these, and as so very little was known about him, he more than captured my interest.

Alan Swain (York), May 2017

Early Life: 1842 to 1874

Henry Hunnings descended from a large South Lincolnshire family which can be traced back to the Middle Ages. In those days it was not unusual for family menfolk to travel south to London in search of work and, with luck, prosperity. Henry's grandfather John Hunnings did exactly that, setting out from his home in South Lincolnshire to take the journey south along Ermine Street (Fig.1) which ran from York to London, passing through Lincolnshire along the way.

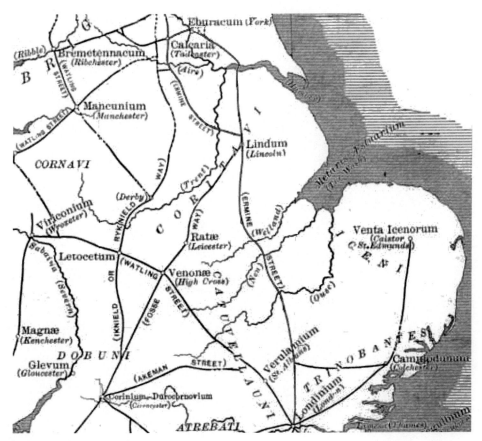

Fig. 1 Ermine Street

At some point on his travels John Hunnings encountered Sarah Langley. They fell in love and were married on 27th October 1788 and set up home together in Tottenham, North London.

The area we know as Tottenham today originated as a ribbon development along the High Road (which was previously the Roman Road called Ermine Street). It was not unusual in those days for newcomers to travel down from the north and settle there.

John and Sarah Hunnings had five children namely Elizabeth, John, March, Samuel and William Butters Hunnings. (March and Butters being names connected with the Lincolnshire Hunnings dynasty). William Butters Hunnings was born on 26th July 1804 but was only 3 years old when father John died at the age of 47 in 1808. This left mother Sarah on her own to bring up the five children.

In the early 19th Century Tottenham was largely a leafy village and at the centre of the Hunnings' family life was All Hallows' Church, Tottenham (Fig.2). William Butters Hunnings married Mary Offwood there on 25th May 1828 and together they had William John (b. 1829), Frederick (b.1833), Alfred (b. 1835) and lastly, on 25th July 1842, their fourth son Henry (Fig. 3). All four sons were baptised at All Hallows but sadly second son Frederick died young, aged 20 months, and was buried in the churchyard.

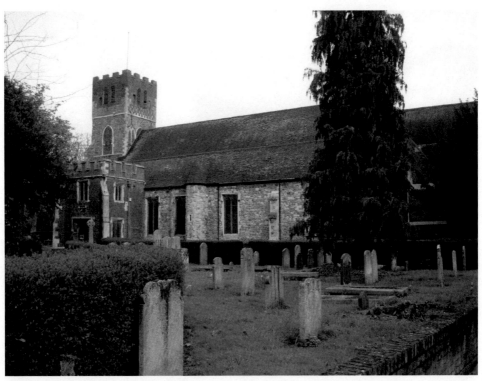

Fig. 2 All Hallows, Tottenham

Page 581

BAPTISMS solemnized in the Parish of Tottenham in the County of Middlesex in the Year 1842.

Page 582

BAPTISMS solemnized in the Parish of Tottenham in the County of Middlesex in the Year 1842

Sold by E. DUNN, Stationer, No. 6, Fleet Street.

Fig. 3 Henry Hunnings Baptism, 1842

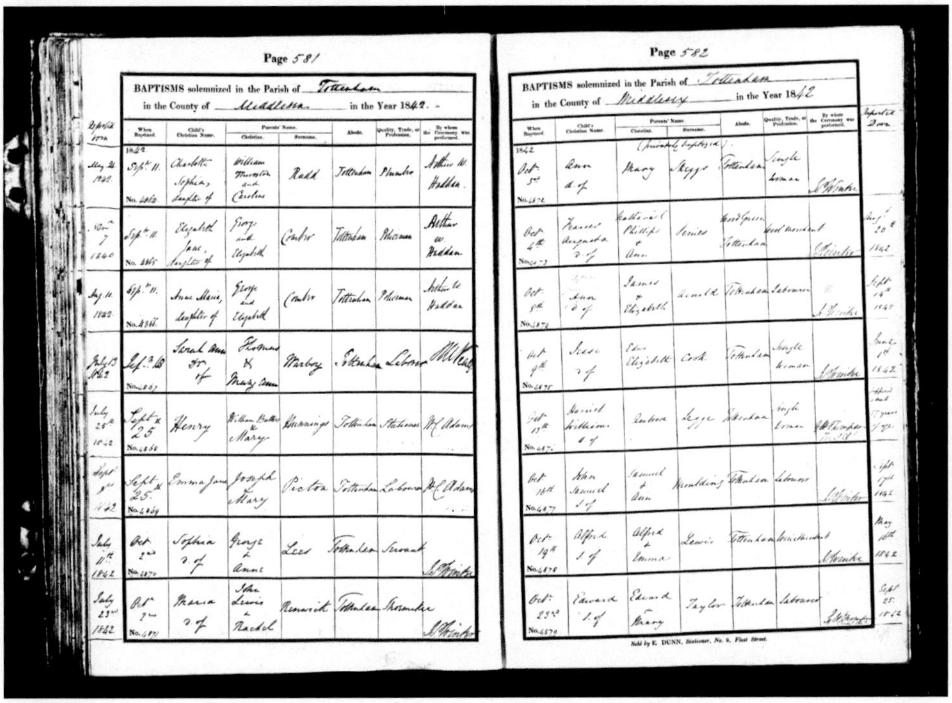

Fig. 4 William Butters Hunnings (Henry's father)

William Butters Hunnings (Fig. 4) was quite an interesting character. In the mid 1820s he established 'Hunnings Printers & Stationers' at 516 High Road, Tottenham (Figs. 5) which he subsequently handed over to eldest son William John in the early 1850s. He became quite a key player within the local community in roles which included Vestry Clerk, Secretary to the Burial Board among others and is well known to the historians of Tottenham. 'Hunnings Printers & Stationers' later moved a short distance to 564 High Road where it remained a local family firm before moving to Finsbury Park in the 1960s.

Fig.5a *516 High Rd, Hunnings Printers and Stationers*

Fig. 5b *516 High Rd. 2016*

Henry Hunnings (Fig. 6) grew up with his father, mother, brothers and grandmother Sarah, living in the rooms above the family business at 516 High Road. Unfortunately, there are no known surviving records of Henry's time at school. However, it would be fair to say he had a good education if evidence from his adult life is to be considered.

Fig. 6 Henry Hunnings, October 1864

Upon leaving school, Henry joined the family 'Printers & Stationers' which was by now registered to 'WJ Hunnings' and being run day to day by Henry's eldest brother William John Hunnings. In the 1861 Census Henry, aged 18, described his occupation as 'Letter Press Printer' and there have survived a few books printed and published by 'WJ Hunnings' during this period, some of which can be found at the British Library (Figs. 7).

Fig. 7a 1861 book

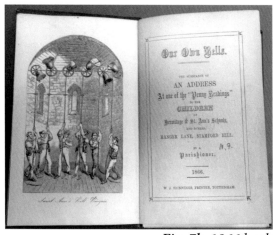

Fig. 7b 1866 book

Significantly though Henry brought his interest and love of photography into the family business enabling 'WJ & H Hunnings' professional photographers to be established. Henry was the principal photographer and a promotional photograph was taken of Henry and elder brother William John to advertise the new line of business (Fig. 8). In those days photography was very much still in its infancy but, ever the pioneer, Henry was at the forefront embracing new ideas and innovations.

Fig. 8 Hunning Bros Photographers

'WJ & H Hunnings' took many photos of local scenes during this time (Figs. 9) but perhaps the most interesting and significant one is a portrait of Hare Pomare. (Fig. 10) Hare Pomare was the son of an important Maori leader in New Zealand. Together with his wife Hariata they were members of a party of Maori people who travelled on a tour to England and were presented to Queen Victoria in July 1863. Whilst in England Hare and his wife stayed some of the time with Elizabeth Fairburn Colenso in Tottenham. Presumably this is where they met the Hunnings family. On 26 October 1863 Hariata gave birth to a son they named Albert Victor, after the Queen and her husband. Subsequently in December 1863 Hare and Hariata visited Queen Victoria at Windsor Castle to present their new son. Queen Victoria was so taken by this she agreed to become Albert Victor's god-mother.

Fig. 9a *Cricketers c1865 (credit WJ and H. Hunnings)*

Fig. 9b *575 High Rd. c1865 (credit WJ and H. Hunnings)*

Fig. 10 Portrait of Hare Pomare 1864 - (credit WJ and H. Hunnings)

The significance of this portrait of Hare Pomare, credited to 'WJ & H Hunnings' and almost certainly taken by Henry Hunnings in January 1864, is that it has now been registered and recorded as the official portrait of Hare Pomare and the original is held at the National Library of New Zealand.

In January 1868, at the 'ripe old age' of 25, Henry left the family business and enrolled as a student at St Edmund Hall, University of Oxford with intent to join the Clergy (Fig. 11).

Fig. 11 St. Edmund Hall

Whilst at Oxford, Hunnings befriended William Luther Leeman, the second son of the esteemed George Leeman of York. William Luther Leeman would also go on to join the Clergy and remained close friends with Hunnings for many years. The two had quite contrasting personalities apparently though as Hunnings was generally shy, quiet, reserved and a Conservative whilst Leeman was confident, outgoing and came from a family of Liberal MPs.

It would not be unreasonable to assume that Hunnings was not an outstanding Oxford scholar but he persevered and eventually earned his Bachelor of Arts degree on 8th December 1870, aged 28.

The following is a transcript from Hunnings' official academic record that was held by Principal Moore who oversaw St Edmund Hall at the time. As can be seen Hunnings didn't pass all his exams at the first attempt.

Hunnings, H
- Entered Jan/68
- Responsions passed Dec/68
- Moderations failed ET/69 passed MT/69
- 2nd Schools Maths failed ET/70
- 2nd Schools Classics & Maths passed Dec 1870
- BA Degree Dec 8, 1870
- To be ordained to curacy at Brighton
- MA – June 18, 1874

(Principal Moore's official notes on H. Hunnings – with grateful thanks to St Edmund Hall, Oxford University for this information)

Upon leaving Oxford University the now Henry Hunnings BA did indeed join the Clergy being ordained as a Deacon in Chichester in 1870, taking up his first position at St Patrick's, Hove, Sussex. The 1871 Census records the fact that Hunnings was still living with his parents at 516 High Road, Tottenham no doubt commuting to St Patrick's as required.

On 26ᵗʰ May 1872 Henry Hunnings was ordained as a Priest by the Bishop of Carlisle with help from receipt of 'letters of dimissory' from William Scott Wilson, the Bishop of Glasgow and Galloway. After a short spell as Curate at Ayr (1872) Hunnings took up residence at 24 Royal Crescent, Glasgow and in 1873 became both Curate at St John, Glasgow and Chaplain to the Bishop of Glasgow and Galloway.

Fig. 12 *Oxford Alumni Record*

As a result of serving four successful years as a 'graduate Curate', Henry Hunnings BA was finally awarded his Master of Arts by the Vice-Chancellor of St Edmund Hall. This special ceremony took place at 11am on June 18th, 1874 in the Sheldonian Theatre, Oxford.

Hunnings' details and achievements are summarised in the official Oxford Alumni Record (Fig.12).

It was now time for the Reverend Henry Hunnings MA (Oxon), age 31, to find a permanent Curate's position and on 15th August 1874 an interesting vacancy for a Curate at Bolton Percy, in the Diocese of York, was advertised.

****

Bolton Percy

Consecrated in 1424, All Saints', Bolton Percy, near York (Fig. 13) was considered a significant Church in the Diocese of York until more recent and modern times. In the late 19th Century

Fig. 13 *All Saints, Bolton Percy*

for the resident priest it was very highly paid too. In 1877, for example, it was recorded as having an annual net income living of £1240. The Vicar at that time was the Venerable Archdeacon of York Rev Stephen Creyke of whom it has been written, turned down a promotion within the Church of England to remain at All Saints'. It has also been written that Rev Creyke was considered something of a 'celebrity vicar' or perhaps the nearest thing to one at that time. Very rarely heard in the pulpit but often seen mingling and socialising with the local dignitaries of the day. Not surprising that he needed two Curates and in the summer of 1874 with the departure of Curate Rev George Wilberforce Trevor one of these positions became vacant.

In his 1899 book 'Memories of a Half Century' Richard William Hiley (then Vicar of Wighill) described Mr. Creyke as

"a man of tall, commanding presence, in fact a very handsome man, and evidently accustomed to "society". He must also have been a scholar, for he took a First Class in classical honours, and was, headmaster of the Boys Grammar School in York. The moment Bolton Percy, the best living in the diocese, was vacant, he is credited with having importuned for that preferment. He had the reputation of being a haughty man towards the "inferior clergy" and such I found to be the case. It was my lot to call upon him as my Archdeacon on business, when he bowed stiffly to me saying: "I have not the pleasure of knowing you, sir," with a pursing of the lip that was peculiar to himself when acting the Grand Seigneur. My reply was: "Is it my fault, sir, if my Archdeacon does not know me?" and I was careful that the knowledge should never be increased".

Rev Stephen Creyke's portrait hangs on the north wall of All Saints', Bolton Percy to this day and he is buried in the Cemetery Garden opposite the Church alongside his wife Sarah. His most renowned lasting legacy to All Saints' is the magnificent East window which he lovingly restored at his own expense in 1866.

So, on 30th October 1874, with a letter of testimonial signed by the Bishop of Glasgow and Galloway and three Glasgow Clergymen (Rev JWW Penney, Rev WR Gallacher and Rev James McCann), together with a nomination from Rev

Stephen Creyke (who incidentally granted Hunnings a healthy stipend of £150 per annum) the Archbishop of York had no problem in giving Henry Hunnings a Licence for the vacant Curate's position at All Saints', Bolton Percy (Fig. 14).

Henry Hunnings must have been on cloud nine to be held in

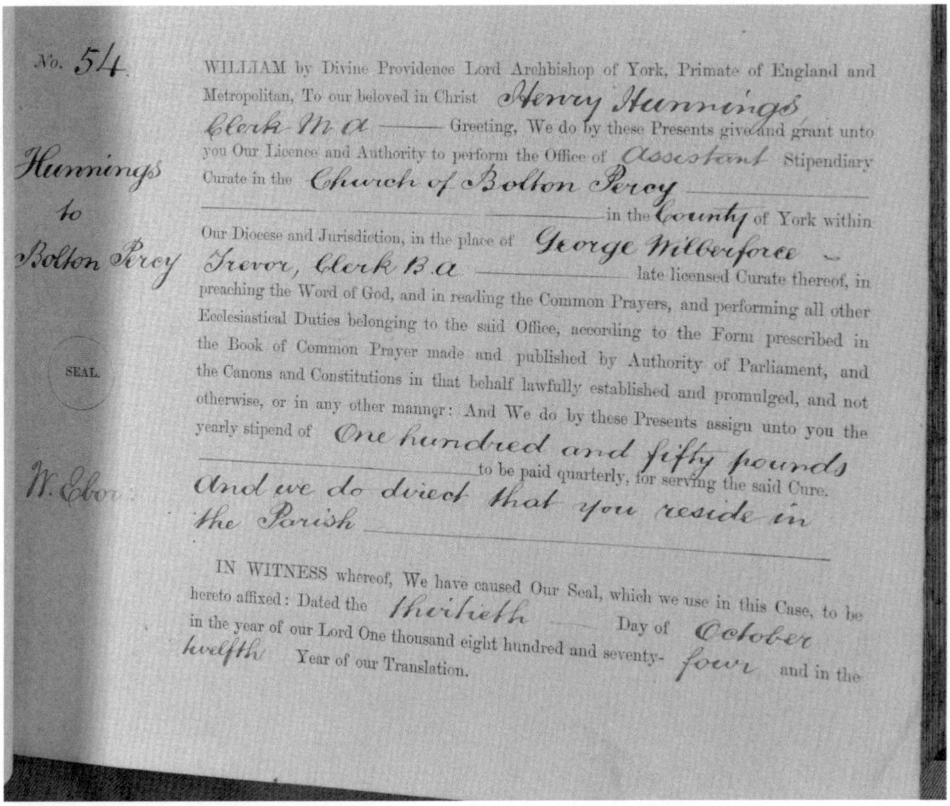

No. 54.

Hunnings to Bolton Percy

SEAL

W. Ebor:

WILLIAM by Divine Providence Lord Archbishop of York, Primate of England and Metropolitan, To our beloved in Christ Henry Hunnings Clerk M A Greeting, We do by these Presents give and grant unto you Our Licence and Authority to perform the Office of Assistant Stipendiary Curate in the Church of Bolton Percy in the County of York within Our Diocese and Jurisdiction, in the place of George Wilberforce Trevor, Clerk B.A late licensed Curate thereof, in preaching the Word of God, and in reading the Common Prayers, and performing all other Ecclesiastical Duties belonging to the said Office, according to the Form prescribed in the Book of Common Prayer made and published by Authority of Parliament, and the Canons and Constitutions in that behalf lawfully established and promulged, and not otherwise, or in any other manner: And We do by these Presents assign unto you the yearly stipend of One hundred and fifty pounds to be paid quarterly, for serving the said Cure. And we do direct that you reside in the Parish

IN WITNESS whereof, We have caused Our Seal, which we use in this Case, to be hereto affixed: Dated the Thirtieth Day of October in the year of our Lord One thousand eight hundred and seventy-four and in the twelfth Year of our Translation.

Fig. 14 Henry Hunnings' Licence - All Saints, Bolton Percy

such high esteem by these important members of the Clergy and to land such a prime and distinguished, not to mention well paid, position. I'm sure the Hunnings family back home in Tottenham were very proud indeed of their youngest brother and son at this time.

And so it was that the Rev Henry Hunnings MA, age 32,

arrived in Bolton Percy and took up residence in The Rectory (Fig. 15) with the Rev Creyke and family and the various servants who worked there.

Fig. 15 *Old Rectory, Bolton Percy*

Hunnings' first recorded key activity as a Curate at All Saints' was on November 28th 1874 when he conducted the burial of Fanny Fawcett. One activity he also carried out whilst at All Saints' was to maintain the Account Book for the Parish Charities and he seemed to enjoy keeping and maintaining records, being a clerk, much like his father. (Note: Hunnings seemingly never aspired to become a Vicar with his own Parish. It appeared he preferred instead to remain in the background in a more supporting role as a Curate and clerk).

There is a Kelly's Directory record from 1877 still in existence which showed Hunnings in Bolton Percy living at the Rectory and working alongside fellow Curate Thomas Smith. A copy of the All Saints' Parish Baptism Register from that period shows both Curates fully active together with Rev England the resident Curate at nearby Appleton Roebuck (Fig. 16).

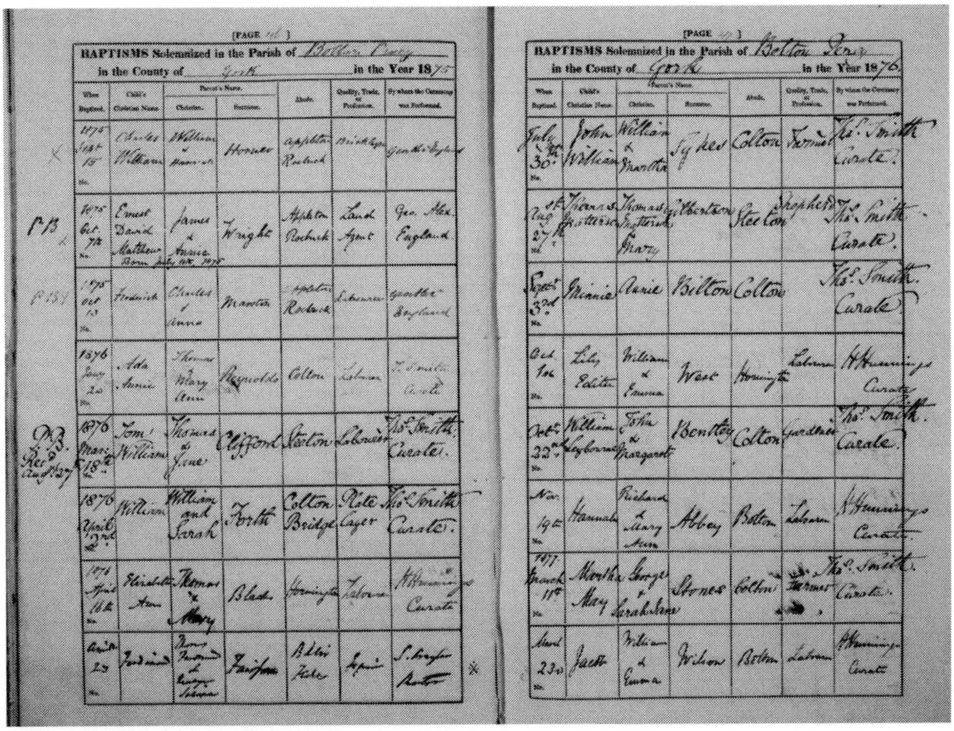

Fig. 16 Bolton Percy Baptisms 1875 - 77

However, they were not given the responsibility for the Baptism of the unfortunate Ferdinand Fairfax, son of Lt-Col Thomas Ferdinand Fairfax, in April 1876. That service was taken by Archdeacon Creyke instead. (Note: Ferdinand Fairfax [b. 22nd March 1876] died on 14th July 1876, aged 4 months, and was buried at St James Church, Bilbrough).

Now, also at that time in Great Britain, there was something of a technology revolution under way, brought about by science and improvements in engineering. The "western world" was leading the way and was full of entrepreneurs and inventors.

Thomas Edison and Alexander Graham Bell were two such prime examples.

Henry Hunnings, who already had a keen interest in the developments of photography, had also become very interested in the emergence of telephony. The telephone had been launched and announced to the world in 1876 by Alexander Graham Bell, a Scot now living in America. The component parts of Bell's original telephone invention were very basic and crude. The original transmitter, for example, was water based and not portable. In 1877 Thomas Edison, an American, invented a telephone transmitter which utilised a solid lump of carbon behind two pressure plates but although it worked and was portable, was noisy and a long way from perfect. Hunnings clearly thought he could do better.

In his spare time, Hunnings began to experiment using a box 2 feet long with a paper lid. He laid a line of cinders on top of the lid and connected an electrode to each end. He connected a battery to the electrodes and found that when he spoke toward the cinders he could hear his voice being transmitted. Over time he perfected this experiment using crushed up engine coke which he collected from Bolton Percy Station goods yard, using tinfoil as a diaphragm and a small 2" diameter wooden tube. This produced a much clearer voice signal. He made further changes and improvements to the design until he had a good working model. (Note: for a detailed description of the transmitter see Appendix 1).

And so, at the age of 36, and whilst still fulfilling his Curacy duties at Bolton Percy, Hunnings patented his telephone transmitter design in the UK. Patent No. 3647 was granted to

Henry Hunnings, of Bolton Percy, in the County of York, for the Invention of "IMPROVEMENTS IN AND APPERTAINING TO TRANSMITTERS FOR TELEPHONES, Sealed the 24th December 1878 and dated 16th September 1878" (Figs. 17).

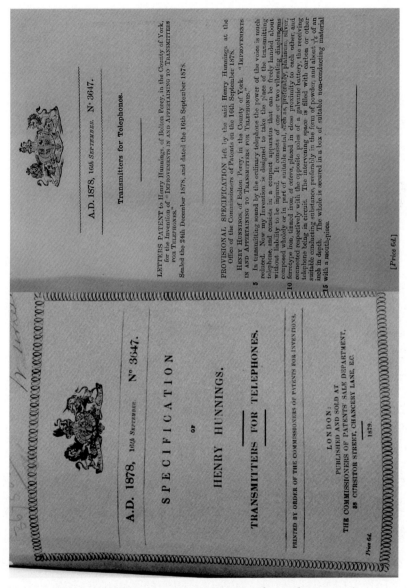

Fig. 17a UK Patent 3647 (extract from document)

Fig. 17b *UK Patent No. 3647 Announced in London Gazette*

1879 was a pivotal year in the life of Rev Henry Hunnings. He was still carrying out Church duties as required but his telephone transmitter had begun to make a significant impact on his life. He had befriended a local engineer, Edward Cox Walker, who shared Hunnings' interest in the telephone but, in contrast, Cox Walker had the means to do something about it.

Edward Cox Walker (b.1838) had served an apprenticeship as a telegraph operator and became a telegraph superintendent for the railways but from 1868 changed tack and worked at Thomas Cooke & Sons, an astronomical instrument makers in York. Like Hunnings, he had followed the development of the telephone closely and had even designed a workable receiver but his ambition was more along commercial lines. Cox Walker, together with Edward Harrison, formed 'Harrison, Cox Walker and Co.' in Darlington and their plan was to specialise in telephone/signalling systems and construction.

In 1879 'Harrison, Cox Walker and Co.' transformed Henry Hunnings' Patent No.3647 into a manufactured product and they called it the 'Hunnings Micro-telephone', priced at 15 guineas (Fig. 18).

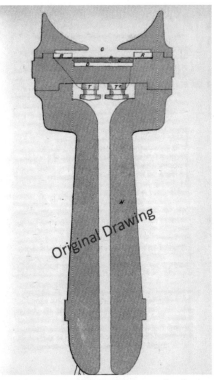

Fig. 18 Hunnings Micro-telephone

One can only speculate how Henry Hunnings felt when he woke from his sleep on 25th July 1879, his 37th Birthday, but one could imagine him feeling positive and excited. He had a privileged posting in the clergy, was the inventor of a device that enabled him to rub shoulders with the likes of Bell and Edison and now had a manufactured piece of telephone equipment with his name on it. His dream of doing something and being someone were beginning to become a reality.

Throughout the remainder of 1879 Hunnings gave public demonstrations of the Micro-telephone device at a series of events throughout Yorkshire and he was even awarded a medal at the prestigious Yorkshire Fine Art & Industrial Exhibition in October of that year. But he still had time to deliver a "most impressive sermon" at the Harvest Thanksgiving Service at Kirkby Wharfe on Sunday 9th November 1879 which was reported locally.

Rev Henry Hunnings MA served the people of Bolton Percy for almost 6 years. During that time he conducted 12 baptisms, 18 burials and 8 marriages as well as keeping the church books and finances in good order. Not a huge amount of effort for £150pa but he undoubtedly worked hard in his spare time perfecting his telephone transmitter invention.

Today only one gravestone remains from all of the Hunnings led burials at All Saints'. The final resting place of Ann Abbey who died on 16th and whose Burial took place on 19th December 1878 is still evident in Bolton Percy Cemetery Garden although not that much of the gravestone has survived (Fig. 19).

Sadly, however, all was not well in his world and as 1880 approached Rev Henry Hunnings was harbouring a secret from which he would never fully recover. It would cause him to leave Bolton Percy and put his life on hold for a period whilst he worked out an escape route and a forward plan that would enable him to get his life back on track.

Fig. 19 *Grave of Ann Abbey, Bolton Percy Cemetery Garden*

Margaret Ann Ridley

Margaret Ann Ridley was the ninth child of Edmund and Catherine Ridley. The Ridley family, originally from Cumbria, had lived for many years at Ferry House near the old (second) church in Bishopthorpe, near York. Father Edmund and mother Catherine were typical working people of the day and had a large family, with eleven children. Edmund Ridley was a coachman and in the mid-to-late 1870s he moved with his family from Bishopthorpe to one of the cottages near All Saints' Church in Bolton Percy. By this time though, the eight older children had grown up and moved on leaving just the three youngest children Margaret, Alfred and James at home with their parents.

Despite the older children having left home and moved away there still remained a close bond particularly between the women of the family. (Note: upon their passing both Edmund and Catherine Ridley were buried in the Cemetery Garden at Bolton Percy).

How and when exactly Margaret met Henry Hunnings we will never know. Most likely Margaret worked at The Rectory as a Housemaid or in some other similar role in the village but it is of no great significance. What is significant though is that in the late summer of 1879 the young 18-year-old Margaret Ridley became pregnant to 37-year-old, Rev Henry Hunnings MA (Oxon) Photographer, Inventor and Curate of the Parish.

This was clearly unexpected and unplanned and one wonders, at a time when everything was going so well for Hunnings, just what impact and distress the realisation of his situation and predicament would have upon him. Clearly if Henry and Margaret were to avoid a scandal they would need to act fast.

Without haste, the pregnant Margaret was sent away to stay with her elder sister Joan (now Joan Miles). Joan who was herself pregnant at the time was married to husband John Miles and living 150 miles away at Wolverton, Buckinghamshire.

With Margaret safely out of sight this gave Henry some time to think about a plan and so, for a short while but with the clock ticking, Hunnings' life in Bolton Percy, on the surface, continued as normal.

Meanwhile Hunnings' friend from University William Luther Leeman was also having problems of his own. Leeman had become the new Vicar at St Thomas, Seaforth, West Lancashire but seemingly some church officials and members of his new congregation were not happy with the way he worked or with some of the decisions he was making.

So Leeman was also a man under pressure and by December 1879, as the year drew to a close, it would be reasonable to say both men were in need of some good fortune.

The fast approaching year 1880 would prove to be a significant year for Henry Hunnings as he tried desperately hard to avoid any scandal. Undoubtedly his predicament greatly upset him and it is arguable he never fully recovered. What follows are the key events that happened in that year.

1880; A Year of Upheaval and Change

On 4th January 1880 Rev Henry Hunnings conducted what would be his final baptism at All Saints', Bolton Percy, that of Emily Gekhill. Three weeks later on 26th January Augustus Duncombe, the Dean of York, passed away at the age of 65.

While the City of York was still in shock at the sudden passing of their beloved Dean, on the 27th January 1880, Hunnings, together with Edward Harrison and Edward Cox Walker, carried out a public demonstration of the Hunnings Micro-telephone. This was between York and Darlington stations, a distance of approximately 45 miles. Two telephones were connected to the telegraph wires that ran alongside the railway, one at each end. Songs were sung, numbers and the alphabet were recited and pretend railway messages were transmitted between the two stations, and received with clarity. This event, which was widely reported in the press at that time, (Fig. 20) was arranged with the co-operation of the Chairman of the North Eastern Railway, George Leeman, the father of Hunnings' friend William Luther Leeman.

> THE NORTHERN ECHO, THURSDAY, JANUARY 29, 1880.
>
> THE TELEPHONE AT DARLINGTON.—On Tuesday evening, by permission of Mr Gray, Chief Telegraph Engineer of the North-Eastern Railway Company, Mr E. Harrison, of Darlington (of the firm of Harrison and Son, jewellers), tried a pair of Hunning's micro telephones on the telegraph wires of the company. The distance is forty-four miles between Bank Top Station, Darlington, and York. The experiment was successful in every way, and conversations, songs, &c., were kept up for an hour by a large number of railway officials and friends.

Fig. 20 Northern Echo - Telephone Experiment report

On 6th of February 1880 the funeral of the Dean of York took place. There was a huge turn out with hundreds lining the streets of York and also at York Station where a special train was waiting to take the Dean to Helmsley, his final resting place. A great many local York clergymen were present and it is highly likely that Hunnings was there along with other representatives from Bolton Percy. The occasion was a sombre one and amongst the members of the clergy who had travelled some distance to pay their last respects was Rev William Luther Leeman.

This gave both men the opportunity to come together on the day to confide in each other and work out a plan that would help them address their problems. The solution they came up with would not be executed for several weeks but undoubtedly Hunnings had one eye on the vacant Curate's post at Holy Trinity, Rothwell, near Leeds, which was advertised on 28th February 1880.

March 1880 was a significant month. Hunnings conducted his final All Saints' Bolton Percy Burial on 3rd (Elizabeth Holmes) and his final Marriage Ceremony on Monday 8th (Owen Maltby and Emma Varley (Fig. 21)). And then, that very week, Henry Hunnings left Bolton Percy. We will never know just exactly how dramatic Hunnings' departure was or indeed under what terms he left his job there but one could imagine it to be emotional and possibly sudden with very little notice. After all, Archdeacon Creyke and other dignitaries including the Bishop of Glasgow had vouched for Hunnings' "good character and high moral standards" in their letters of nomination to the Archbishop. Getting a young girl pregnant out of wedlock was clearly not in their thinking.

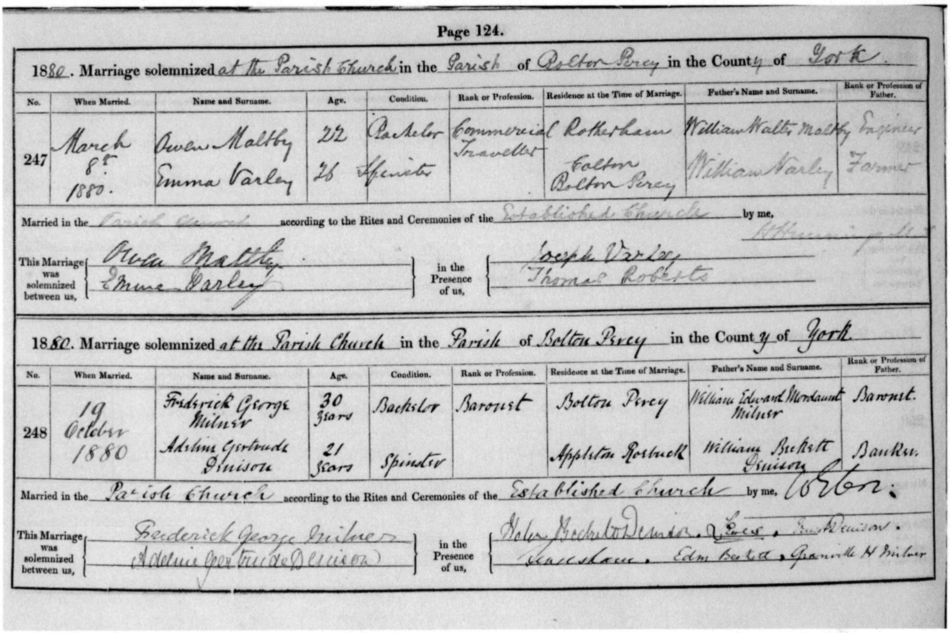

Fig. 21 *Marriage of Owen Maltby and Emma Varley, March 1880*

Another high-profile demonstration of the Hunnings Micro-telephone was given to the esteemed Cleveland Institution of Engineers (CIE) during the evening of Monday 15th March 1880 (Fig. 22). This took place at the offices of Messrs Stevens, Jacques and Co. in Middlesbrough but significantly Hunnings was absent and Edward Harrison took his place. Edward Cox Walker was at the other end of their private wire at the Acklam Works just a few miles away. Conversation and songs were transmitted between the two and received with "decided success" prompting laughter from the gentlemen assembled to which Cox Walker replied from the other end with "Don't laugh so loud, please!"

Mar. 15th, 1880
Paper on "The Cleveland Ironstone," by Mr George Barrow, F.G.S.
H.M. Geological survey. (Note that there is a second part to
this paper presented at the May meeting of this session)

"Description of Hunnings' micro-telephone," by Mr E. Harrison,
Darlington, with experiments at Messrs Stevenson, Jacques and
Co.'s Offices.

Fig. 22 CIE Meeting - 15th March 1880

But then on 18th March 1880 Henry "did the right thing" and married Margaret Ann Ridley, who was by now seven months pregnant. They were married at St George the Martyr, Wolverton the local parish church near to where Margaret had been staying with sister Joan and her husband John Miles since becoming pregnant. This explains Hunnings' absence from the telephone demonstration to the CIE three days before. At that time, the CIE were an influential industrial and academic body in the North of England and Hunnings would have most definitely wanted to be present and leading the demonstration.

On the marriage certificate (Fig. 23) Margaret Ridley recorded her address as Wolverton, whilst Henry Hunnings recorded his as Tottenham. Interestingly neither of them mentioned Bolton Percy. Hunnings also stated his profession as simply 'Clerk' with no mention of his role in the Clergy.

GIVEN AT THE GENERAL REGISTER OFFICE

Application Number 6965149-1

No.	When Married.	Name and Surname.	Age.	Condition.	Rank or Profession.	Residence at the time of Marriage.	Father's Name and Surname.	Rank or Profession of Father.
135 18	*1872.* March 18/80.	Henry Hunnings Margaret Ann Ridley	37 19	Bachelor Spinster	Clerk —	Attenborough, Weaverton	William Butler Hunnings Edmund Ridley	Vestry Clerk Coachman

Married in the _____ Above Church _____ according to the Rites and Ceremonies of the Established Church, by _____ licence _____ by me,

This Marriage was solemnized between us,

{ Henry Hunnings
  Margaret Ann Ridley }

in the Presence of us,

{ Benjamin Franklin ...
  Rebecca Giles }

CERTIFIED to be a true copy of an entry in the certified copy of a register of Marriages in the Registration District of **Potterspury**

Given at the GENERAL REGISTER OFFICE, under the Seal of the said Office, the **30th** day of **November** **2015**

MXG 676685

Fig. 23 Henry Hunnings' Marriage Certificate

The marriage was witnessed by John Miles and Benjamin Franklin. (This Benjamin Franklin was not the famous American forefather and inventor, instead he was a local Wolverton schoolteacher and St George the Martyr church clerk). There is no evidence that any Hunnings family members were present, only Ridley family members seemingly attended.

One might conclude they didn't want anyone back at Bolton Percy or Tottenham to know of their predicament.

After the wedding Margaret, heavily pregnant, returned to York to stay with another sister. This time it was with sister Mary (now married and called Mary Foster) who was living at 9 Nunthorpe Road (Fig. 24). It is not clear if Henry accompanied Margaret on this long journey as he instead took up temporary residence in Seaforth, close to his friend William Luther Leeman's Church.

Fig. 24 9, Nunthorpe Road, York

At the St Thomas, Seaforth Annual Vestry Meeting on 30th March 1880 things came to a head for Rev William Luther Leeman and he had to vigorously defend against his critics in this very public meeting. Amongst other accusations he denied being one of "the dangerous men".

So in April 1880 Leeman took a three-month sabbatical and went to London. He subsequently handed over the reins at St Thomas temporarily to Canon J. C. Ryle (who was in line to become the new Bishop of Liverpool) with Rev Henry Hunnings as his Curate. A convenient solution that would give both Hunnings and Leeman some respite from their recent troubles.

During the late 1870s the telephone market in the UK had been dominated by Bell and Edison and both had formed British based companies which were locked in bitter opposition to each other. The threat by the British Post Office, who ran the UK telegraph network, to take over all telephony in the UK caused the two tycoons to form a united front. So, on 13th May 1880, they joined forces and together they launched the United Telephone Company Ltd (UTC Ltd) (Fig. 25).

Fig. 25 UTC Ltd Head Office, London

Meanwhile, Harrison, Cox Walker & Co had begun manufacturing telephone instruments and businesses were buying them. One such example was reported in The Sunderland Daily Echo in May 1880 whereby a company called 'Ferens & Love' had purchased and installed the Hunnings/Cox-Walker equipment and were successfully using it between their premises at Durham and Cornsay.

On 24th May 1880 Margaret gave birth to a son, at her sister Mary's home (9 Nunthorpe Road, York). Margaret once again using her 'sisterhood' for help. Henry and Margaret named the new boy William Butters Hunnings after Henry's father but the birth would not be registered until almost a year later. It is extremely unlikely that Hunnings was present at the birth as he was active at St Thomas, Seaforth, between early May and July of that year.

Then in July 1880 things would change once again. Leeman's sabbatical in London was coming to an end and so Henry moved back to Yorkshire to help Rev George Heberden at Holy Trinity, Rothwell (Fig. 26) who was still without a Curate.

Fig. 26 Holy Trinity, Rothwell near Leeds

On 18th July 1880 Rev Henry Hunnings conducted the Baptism of Hannah Harrand at Holy Trinity, Rothwell, and immediately thereafter got to work. Margaret and new baby William Butters joined Henry and they took up residence in nearby Woodlesford.

After a few months of hard work Rev Henry Hunnings must have impressed as on 9th December 1880 Rev George Heberden formally wrote a letter of nomination to the Bishop of Ripon for Hunnings to be his new Curate.

Rev John Greenwood Smith (Vicar of Christ Church, Hunslet, Leeds) who also knew Hunnings from University, together with Rev Philip Yorke Savile (Rector of Methley) and Rev Robert Chadwick (Vicar of Christ Church, Lofthouse) provided the necessary letter of testimonial in support.

The Bishop of Ripon duly approved and on 29th December 1880 Rev Henry Hunnings MA was officially licensed as the new Curate at Holy Trinity, Rothwell and for a while things settled down. Interestingly Hunnings had to work much harder for his £150 per annum stipend at Holy Trinity and by the time he left a year later had presided over 88 Baptisms, 72 Burials and 8 Marriages – collectively over 4 times as many events and in 4 less years than at Bolton Percy!

A Fresh Start

For the majority of 1881 Henry Hunnings was kept busy with his church duties at Holy Trinity and was fairly low-key outside of his Curacy apart from giving a few telephone lectures. He also decided to further protect his carbon-granule telephone transmitter invention in August 1881, whilst he was working at Rothwell, by patenting it in the United States of America.

Then toward the end of 1881 things changed for the young Hunnings family as they relocated to Ryde, Isle of Wight (Fig. 27), in other words, about as far away from Yorkshire as possible! Henry even wrote a letter of commendation to the Isle of Wight Observer for the removal company 'Messrs Curtiss & Sons'.

Extract from The Isle of Wight Observer; Saturday January 14th 1882

Fig. 27 Ryde Directory, 1882

39

At the age of 39 Rev Henry Hunnings became the new Curate at All Saints, Ryde, (Fig. 28) on the picturesque Isle of Wight working for the Rev Alexander Poole. Rev Poole was considered by some at the time to be a difficult man who could be forthright and opinionated. Letters of criticism aimed at Rev Poole were not an uncommon feature in local newspapers and in some cases were even written by fellow members of the Clergy.

Fig. 28 *All Saints, Ryde*

From the heady heights in 1874 working with the Bishop of Glasgow and Galloway followed by Archdeacon Creyke at Bolton Percy the road via Seaforth and Rothwell to the one in 1882 working with the prickly Rev Poole at Ryde was undoubtedly a downhill one for Rev Henry Hunnings. Sadly, and unfortunately, things would not improve and his standing as an inventor was also about to come into question too.

Bell and Edison, through their United Telephone Company Ltd, were attempting to eliminate any form of competition and were bringing about law-suits against competitors or anyone they thought had copied their ideas. They were relentless. So, unsurprisingly, by 1882 UTC Ltd had got Harrison, Cox Walker & Co in their sights alleging infringement of patents for the instruments they had used in their new Hunnings Micro-telephone systems. Bell's main objection was to Cox Walker's receiver but Edison, more significantly for Hunnings, objected to the carbon-granule transmitter on the grounds that it was a copy of his own solid-carbon transmitter invention. Needless to say, Hunnings and Harrison, Cox Walker & Co denied this and so in April 1882 the case went before the High Court in London.

The trial lasted 16 days, but the Judge, Mr. Justice Fry, found in favour of Hunnings stating that Edison's original Patent design was flawed and imperfect. The fall out continued and even played out between UTC Ltd and Hunnings in the 'Letters to Editor' section of The Times where Hunnings also revealed that in 1879 UTC Ltd had approached him with a view to buying his patent. But UTC Ltd weren't done yet and in August 1882 they would be granted the right of appeal.

Henry and Margaret's second child Katherine Mary Hunnings was born in April 1882 at the Hunnings' new home on Melville Street, Ryde, and to all intents and purposes, with the potential scandal two years behind them and 300 miles away, the Rev & Mrs Hunnings had resumed normal service.

Now settled on the Isle of Wight, Hunnings became active in the Ryde Conservative Association giving talks, attending functions and speaking out against the Whigs and Liberals in particular.

In 1882 Hunnings was also back on the Telephone Talk circuit giving presentations mainly around the South of England titled 'Telephone; it's History and Construction'. He also placed a weekly advert in the Isle of Wight Observer offering private tuition for young schoolboys at his home in Melville Street. This was something his predecessor at Ryde also did and seemingly went with the job.

UTC Ltd.'s appeal was heard in January 1883 (Fig. 29), except this time the Appeal Judges found in favour of UTC Ltd citing Lord Brougham's Patent Act of 1835 as the clincher. This, very simply, gave the Intellectual Property rights to the original inventor regardless of how imperfect the design or subsequent improvements.

There was uproar over the decision as it threw the whole position of Inventors/Patent Rights into question. It became something of a landmark case in legal history at that time and was referred to the House of Lords. There subsequently would be a new Patent, Designs and Trade Marks Act produced in 1883 which sought to better clarify and tighten up the rules and eventually common sense would prevail.

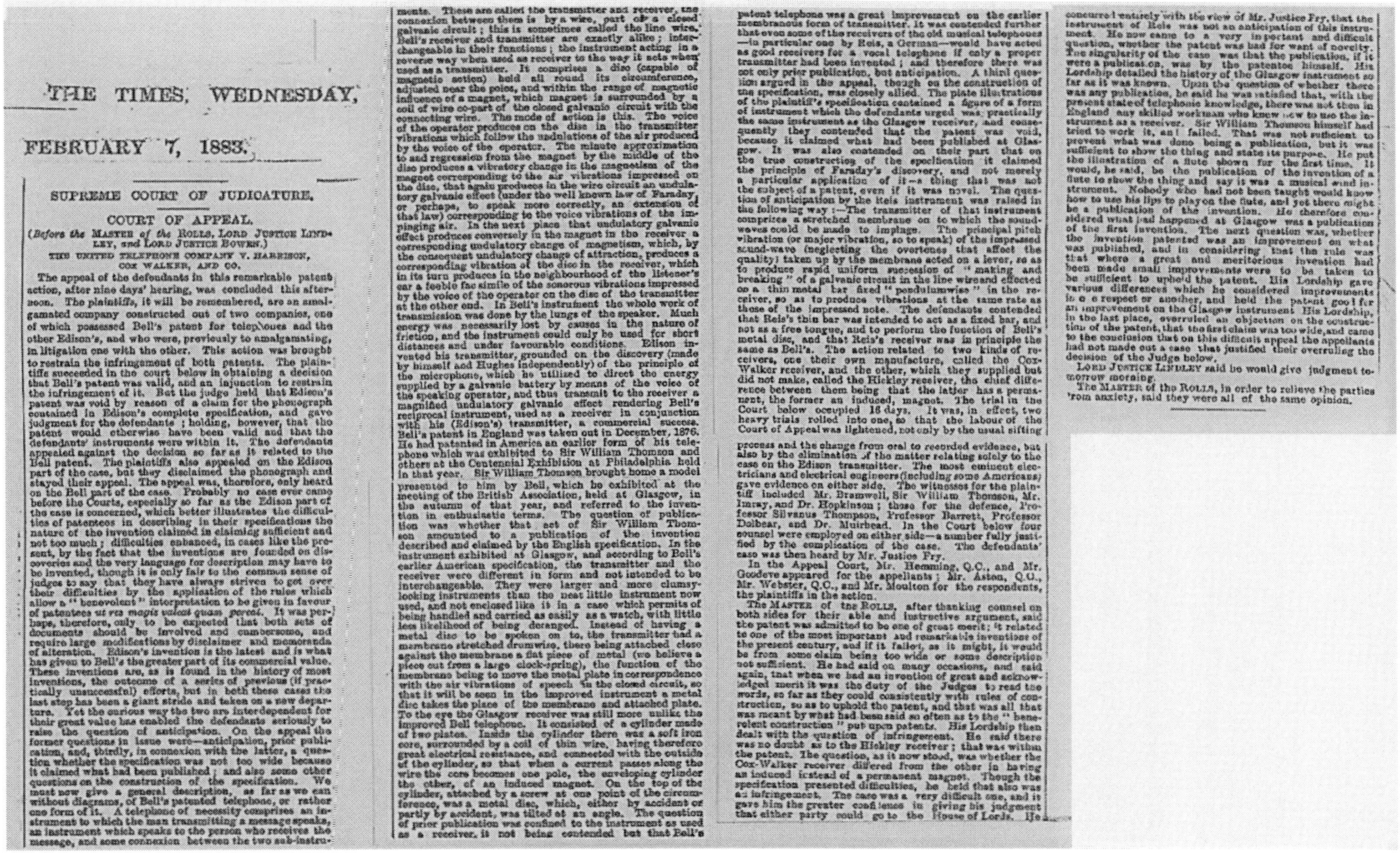

THE TIMES, WEDNESDAY, FEBRUARY 7, 1883.

SUPREME COURT OF JUDICATURE.

COURT OF APPEAL.

(*Before the* MASTER *of the* ROLLS, LORD JUSTICE LINDLEY, *and* LORD JUSTICE BOWEN.)

THE UNITED TELEPHONE COMPANY V. HARRISON, COX WALKER, AND CO.

The appeal of the defendants in this remarkable patent action, after nine days' hearing, was concluded this afternoon. The plaintiffs, it will be remembered, are an amalgamated company constructed out of two companies, one of which possessed Bell's patent for telephones and the other Edison's, and who were, previously to amalgamating, in litigation one with the other. This action was brought to restrain the infringement of both patents. The plaintiffs succeeded in the court below in obtaining a decision that Bell's patent was valid, and an injunction to restrain the infringement of it. But the judge held that Edison's patent was void by reason of a claim for the phonograph contained in Edison's complete specification, and gave judgment for the defendants; holding, however, that the patent would otherwise have been valid and that the defendants' instruments were within it. The defendants appealed against the decision so far as it related to the Bell patent. The plaintiffs also appealed on the Edison part of the case, but they disclaimed the phonograph and stayed their appeal. The appeal was, therefore, only heard on the Bell part of the case. Probably no case ever came before the Courts, especially so far as the Edison part of the case is concerned, which better illustrates the difficulties of patentees in describing in their specifications the nature of the invention claimed in claiming sufficient and not too much; difficulties enhanced, in cases like the present, by the fact that the inventions are founded on discoveries and the very language for description may have to be invented, though it is only fair to the common sense of judges to say that they have always striven to get over their difficulties by the application of the rules which allow a "benevolent" interpretation to be given in favour of patentees *ut res magis valeat quam pereat*. It was perhaps, therefore, only to be expected that both sets of documents should be involved and cumbersome, and require large modifications by disclaimer and memoranda of alteration. Edison's invention is the latest and is what has given to Bell's the greater part of its commercial value. These inventions are, as is found in the history of most inventions, the outcome of a series of previous (if practically unsuccessful) efforts, but in both these cases the last step has been a giant stride and taken on a new departure. Yet the curious way the two are interdependent for their great value has enabled the defendants seriously to raise the question of anticipation. On the appeal the former questions in issue were—anticipation, prior publication, and, thirdly, in connexion with the latter, a question whether the specification was not too wide because it claimed what had been published; and also some other questions on the construction of the specification. We must now give a general description, as far as we can without diagrams, of Bell's patented telephone, or rather one form of it. A telephone of necessity comprises an instrument to which the man transmitting a message speaks, an instrument which speaks to the person who receives the message, and some connexion between the two sub-instruments. These are called the transmitter and receiver, the connexion between them is by a wire, part of a closed galvanic circuit; this is sometimes called the line wire. Bell's receiver and transmitter are exactly alike; interchangeable in their functions; the instrument acting in a reverse way when used as receiver to the way it acts when used as a transmitter. It comprises a disc (capable of magnetic action) held all round its circumference, adjusted near the poles, and within the range of magnetic influence of a magnet, which magnet is surrounded by a coil of wire co-part of the closed galvanic circuit with the connecting wire. The mode of action is this. The voice of the operator produces on the disc in the transmitter vibrations which follow the undulations of the air produced by the voice of the operator. The minute approximation to and regression from the magnet by the middle of the disc produces a vibratory change in the magnetism of the magnet corresponding to the air vibrations impressed on the disc, that again produces in the wire circuit an undulatory galvanic effect (under the well known law of Faraday, or perhaps, to speak more correctly, an extension of that law) corresponding to the voice vibrations of the impinging air. In the next place that undulatory galvanic effect produces conversely in the magnet in the receiver a corresponding undulatory change of magnetism, which, by the consequent undulatory change of attraction, produces a corresponding vibration of the disc in the receiver, which in its turn produces in the neighbourhood of the listener's ear a feeble fac simile of the sonorous vibrations impressed by the voice of the operator on the disc of the transmitter at the other end. In Bell's instrument the whole work of transmission was done by the lungs of the speaker. Much energy was necessarily lost by causes in the nature of friction, and the instrument could only be used for short distances and under favourable conditions. Edison invented his transmitter, grounded on the discovery (made by himself and Hughes independently) of the principle of the microphone, which he utilized to direct the energy supplied by a galvanic battery by means of the voice of the speaking operator, and thus transmit to the receiver a magnified undulatory galvanic effect rendering Bell's reciprocal instrument, used as a receiver in conjunction with his (Edison's) transmitter, a commercial success. Bell's patent in England was taken out in December, 1876. He had patented in America an earlier form of his telephone which was exhibited to Sir William Thomson and others at the Centennial Exhibition at Philadelphia held in that year. Sir William Thomson brought home a model presented to him by Bell, which he exhibited at the meeting of the British Association, held at Glasgow, in the autumn of that year, and referred to the invention in enthusiastic terms. The question of publication was whether that act of Sir William Thomson amounted to a publication of the invention described and claimed by the English specification. In the instrument exhibited at Glasgow, and according to Bell's earlier American specification, the transmitter and the receiver were different in form and not intended to be interchangeable. They were larger and more clumsy-looking instruments than the neat little instrument now used, and not enclosed like it in a case which permits of being handled and carried as easily as a watch, with little less likelihood of being deranged. Instead of having a metal disc to be spoken on to, the transmitter had a membrane stretched drumwise, there being attached close against the membrane a flat piece of metal (we believe a piece cut from a large clock-spring), the function of the membrane being to move the metal plate in correspondence with the air vibrations of speech in the closed circuit, so that it will be seen in the improved instrument a metal disc takes the place of the membrane and attached plate. To the eye the Glasgow receiver was still more unlike the improved Bell telephone. It consisted of a cylinder made of two plates. Inside the cylinder there was a soft iron core, surrounded by a coil of thin wire, having therefore great electrical resistance, and connected with the outside of the cylinder, so that when a current passes along the wire the core becomes one pole, the enveloping cylinder the other, of an induced magnet. On the top of the cylinder, attached by a screw at one point of the circumference, was a metal disc, which, either by accident or partly by accident, was tilted at an angle. The question of prior publication was confined to the instrument as used as a receiver, it not being contended but that Bell's patent telephone was a great improvement on the earlier membranous form of transmitter. It was contended further that even some of the receivers of the old musical telephones —in particular one by Reis, a German—would have acted as good receivers for a vocal telephone if only a proper transmitter had been invented; and therefore there was not only prior publication, but anticipation. A third question argued in the appeal, though on the construction of the specification, was closely allied. The plate illustrations of the plaintiff's specification contained a figure of a form of instrument which the defendants urged was practically the same instrument as the Glasgow receiver, and consequently they contended that the patent was void, because it claimed what had been published at Glasgow. It was also contended on their part that on the true construction of the specification it claimed the principle of Faraday's discovery, and not merely a particular application of it—a thing that was not the subject of a patent, even if it was novel. The question of anticipation by the Reis instrument was raised in the following way:—The transmitter of that instrument comprizes a stretched membrane on to which the sound-waves could be made to impinge. The principal pitch vibration (or major vibration, so to speak) of the impressed sound-wave (neglecting the overtones that affect the quality) taken up by the membrane acted on a lever, so as to produce rapid uniform succession of "making and breaking" of a galvanic circuit in the line wire and effected on a thin metal bar fixed "pendulumwise" in the receiver, so as to produce vibrations at the same rate as those of the impressed note. The defendants contended that Reis's thin bar was intended to act as a fixed bar, and not as a free tongue, and to perform the function of Bell's metal disc, and that Reis's receiver was in principle the same as Bell's. The action related to two kinds of receivers, one their own manufacture, called the Cox-Walker receiver, and the other, which they supplied but did not make, called the Hickley receiver, the chief difference between them being that the latter has a permanent, the former an induced, magnet. The trial in the Court below occupied 18 days. It was, in effect, two heavy trials rolled into one, so that the labour of the Court of Appeal was lightened, not only by the usual sifting process and the change from oral to recorded evidence, but also by the elimination of the matter relating solely to the case on the Edison transmitter. The most eminent electricians and electrical engineers (including some Americans) gave evidence on either side. The witnesses for the plaintiff included Mr. Bramwell, Sir William Thomson, Mr. Imray, and Dr. Hopkinson; those for the defence, Professor Silvanus Thompson, Professor Barrett, Professor Dolbear, and Dr. Muirhead. In the Court below four counsel were employed on either side—a number fully justified by the complication of the case. The defendants' case was then heard by Mr. Justice Fry.

In the Appeal Court, Mr. Hemming, Q.C., and Mr. Goodeve appeared for the appellants; Mr. Aston, Q.C., Mr. Webster, Q.C., and Mr. Moulton for the respondents, the plaintiffs in the action.

The MASTER of the ROLLS, after thanking counsel on both sides for their able and instructive argument, said the patent was admitted to be one of great merit; it related to one of the most important and remarkable inventions of the present century, and if it failed, as it might, it would be from some claim being too wide or some description not sufficient. He had said on many occasions, and said again, that when we had an invention of great and acknowledged merit it was the duty of the Judges to read the words, so far as they could consistently with rules of construction, so as to uphold the patent, and that was all that was meant by what had been said so often as to the "benevolent construction" put upon patents. His Lordship then dealt with the question of infringement. He said there was no doubt as to the Hickley receiver; that was within the patent. The question, as it now stood, was whether the Cox-Walker receiver differed from the other in having an induced instead of a permanent magnet. Though the specification presented difficulties, he held that also was an infringement. The case was a very difficult one, and it gave him the greater confidence in giving his judgment that either party could go to the House of Lords. He concurred entirely with the view of Mr. Justice Fry, that the instrument of Reis was not an anticipation of this instrument. He now came to a very important and difficult question, whether the patent was bad for want of novelty. The singularity of the case was that the publication, if it were a publication, was by the patentee himself. His Lordship detailed the history of the Glasgow instrument so far as it was known. Upon the question of whether there was any publication, he said he was satisfied that, with the present state of telephonic knowledge, there was not then in England any skilled workman who knew how to use the instrument as a receiver. Sir William Thomson himself had tried to work it, and failed. That was not sufficient to prevent what was done being a publication, but it was sufficient to show the thing and state its purpose. He put the illustration of a flute shown for the first time. It would, he said, be the publication of the invention of a flute to show the thing and say it was a musical wind instrument. Nobody who had not been taught would know how to use his lips to play on the flute, and yet there might be a publication of the invention. He therefore considered what had happened at Glasgow was a publication of the first invention. The next question was, whether the invention patented was an improvement on what was published, and in considering that the rule was that where a great and meritorious invention had been made small improvements were to be taken to be sufficient to uphold the patent. His Lordship gave various differences which he considered improvements in one respect or another, and held the patent good for an improvement on the Glasgow instrument. His Lordship, in the last place, overruled an objection on the construction of the patent, that the first claim was too wide, and came to the conclusion that on this difficult appeal the appellants had not made out a case that justified their overruling the decision of the Judge below.

LORD JUSTICE LINDLEY said he would give judgment to-morrow morning.

The MASTER of the ROLLS, in order to relieve the parties from anxiety, said they were all of the same opinion.

Fig. 29 The Times report from the Court of Appeal

Too late now though for Henry Hunnings. He finally relented and agreed to sell his carbon-granule telephone transmitter patent to UTC Ltd, where it would soon become their transmitter of choice. He also agreed to appear on Edison's behalf as an 'expert witness' in court cases where infringements of transmitters were alleged.

On 5th February 1884, aged 41, Henry Hunnings was elected to the Ryde Conservative Association Committee after a ballot but by 1885 his health was in decline.

****

Declining Health

After enduring three years with Rev Poole on the Isle of Wight the Rev Henry Hunnings, aged 42, moved back to the mainland with his family and in April 1885 he took over as Curate at St Mary's, Eling, near Southampton (Fig. 30). He would only be there for a brief period but was popular, well-liked and very much involved in the local community. Even wife Margaret helped trim up St Mary's for the 1885 Harvest Festival service.

Fig. 30 St Mary's, Eling

But then the real problems started. In October 1885 and in poor health Hunnings left Eling to become Chaplain of South Hants Infirmary. The Hunnings family were by now living at 20 Carlton Road, Southampton (Fig. 31) which was only a short distance away from the hospital. This position was ratified in January 1886 by the Hospital Board of Governors but sadly, shortly after, Hunnings' health had deteriorated to the point where he could not fully maintain his duties there.

Fig. 31 20, Carlton Road, Southampton

And so, fatefully, on 4th May 1886 Hunnings was asked to resign his position at the Infirmary by Dr Wade who had been sent by the Hospital Governors to see Hunnings at his home and deliver the message. Somewhat ironically it was Dr Wade who had been treating Hunnings for his deteriorating illness which was recorded at the time as "blood on the lungs".

After the meeting with Dr Wade, Hunnings in desperation sought out a colleague (Rev W W Perrin) and asked him to cover the role at the Hospital temporarily until he was in better health. Unfortunately Rev Perrin was not able to help out and the Hospital Governors were emphatic in their decision. Hunnings was devastated by this and called the situation his "death-blow".

One can only speculate on Hunnings' state of mind and reasoning at this time. It could have been his failing health, the shame and consequences of losing his job, the stress of the court cases, his secret regarding Margaret and their first child, or quite possibly a combination of all of these, but we will never know. However, the stark facts are that later that evening he retired to the bedroom and took his own life. His Death Certificate (Fig. 32) states "Died from the effects of prussic acid or one of its compounds, self-administered, of unsound mind".

There was subsequently an inquest and quite a detailed report produced. The verdict given was "suicide while in an unsound state of mind". It was widely reported at that time in the local newspapers (Fig. 33).

It was a tragic and sad end to a talented life but perhaps in some ways sadder still is that in those days suicide was seen as 'self-murder' and therefore a sin. In fact, before the Suicide Act 1961, it was a crime to commit suicide, and anyone who attempted and failed could be prosecuted and imprisoned, while the families of those who succeeded could also potentially be prosecuted.

The Clergy would not allow a self-murderer to be buried on consecrated ground so they were often buried in unmarked graves in municipal cemeteries. This ruling applied to everyone, including members of the Clergy, and because of this there is no apparent lasting record of the final resting place of Henry Hunnings and so it remains, as yet, unknown.

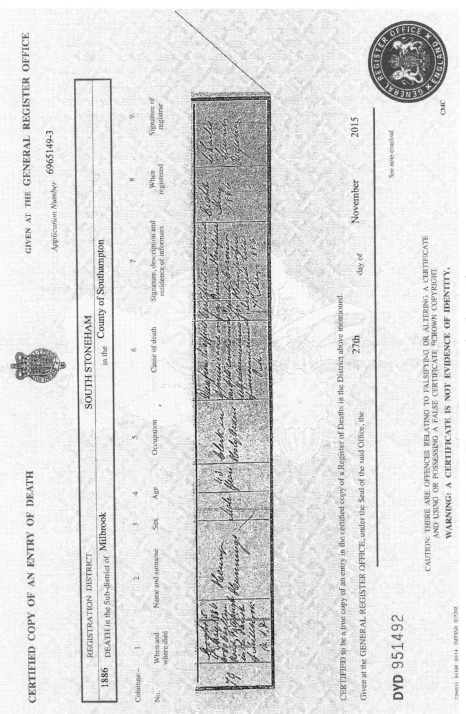

Fig. 32 Henry Hunnings death certificate

48

THE SUICIDE OF A CLERGYMAN

at Southampton formed the subject of a coroner's inquiry on Friday evening.

The Rev. Henry Hunnings, chaplain to the Royal South Hants infirmary, and formerly curate of Eling, Hants, and Ryde, Isle of Wight, had been suffering from hemorrhage of the lungs.

On Tuesday he was unofficially informed that the governors of the infirmary had decided to request him to resign, and that failing his refusal he would be dismissed. This preyed upon his mind very much, and he said it would be his death-blow.

His conduct became strange through the day, and he struck his wife, with whom he had always been on the best of terms, and also his child. Towards evening he went to his bedroom, and sent his wife to order some oysters for supper. When she returned in a short time he was lying on the bed insensible, and he died in a few minutes.

The *post mortem* examination showed that he had taken a considerable quantity of cyanide of potassium, which he had in his possession for use in amateur photography. A verdict of "Suicide in an unsound state of mind" was returned.

Fig. 33 The Cornishman article - Suicide of a Clergyman

Life after Henry

After the shock of Henry's sudden death Margaret wasted no time in bringing her affairs to order, clearly with no means of supporting herself and having two small children to raise on her own. At 1pm on 8th July 1886 there was an auction of household items at the home (20 Carlton Road, Southampton) which Margaret organised through local auctioneers Hunt & Bance.

There was an extensive list of items for sale which included furniture, two drawing room suites, a music Canterbury, walnut and inlaid tables, Brussels carpets, pedestal writing desk, mahogany bagatelle board, hall chairs and table, bedroom effects including wire mattresses and iron bedsteads, washstands with marble tops, a complete set of photographic equipment, a pianoforte and a harmonium (Henry Hunnings was an accomplished pianist and records exist of accounts of him playing the organ and harmonium in church). A surprisingly large number of items for a Curate's modest home although no mention of any telephone equipment, experimental or otherwise.

Clearly the sale had some success as by 28th July 1886 initial details of the estate were published with a total estate value of £811 17s 6d. That sum was revised upwards to £1222 12s 6d in March 1887 (Fig. 34). Quite a considerable sum for a Curate to leave behind.

In October 1887 Margaret Hunnings re-married and was

very soon pregnant with her third child. Her new husband was Mr John Montague Wood-Taylor. Wood–Taylor came from a wealthy Nottinghamshire family who also had links to Scarborough, Leeds and Harrogate. Wood-Taylor never appeared to have a job of any kind as all his recorded documents stated "living by own means" or similar wording.

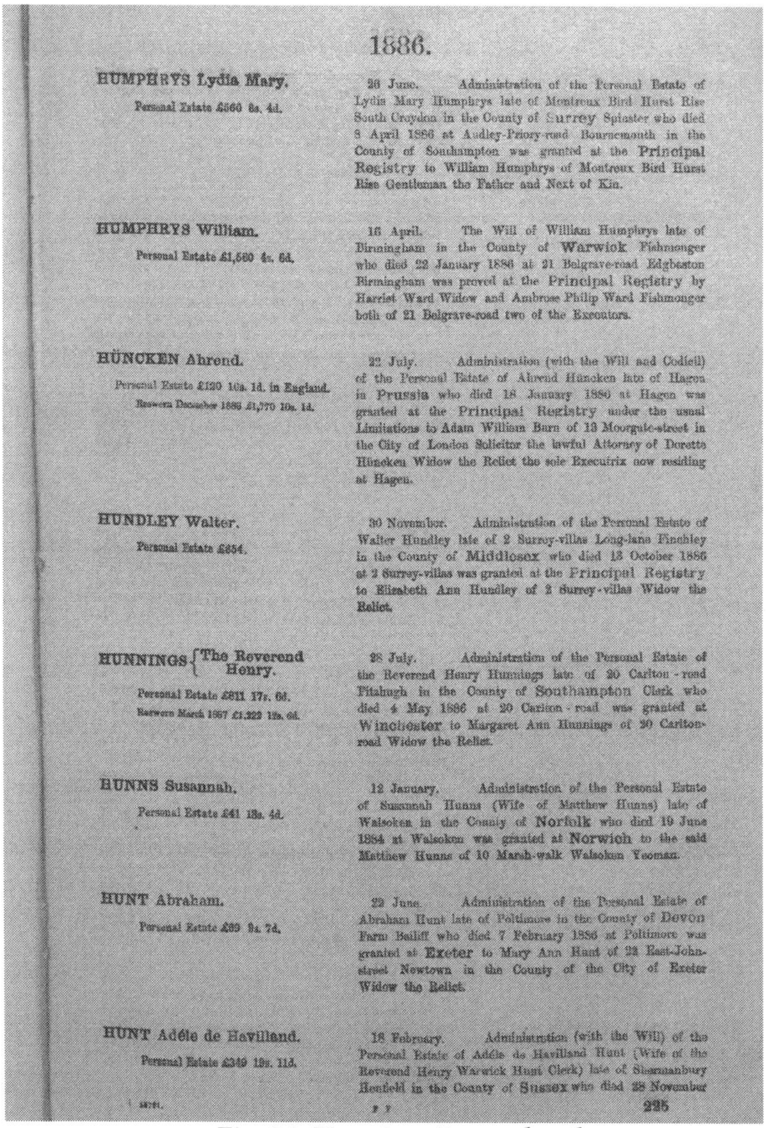

1886.

HUMPHRYS Lydia Mary.
Personal Estate £560 8s. 4d.

26 June. Administration of the Personal Estate of Lydia Mary Humphrys late of Montreux Bird Hurst Rise South Croydon in the County of Surrey Spinster who died 8 April 1886 at Audley-Priory-road Bournemouth in the County of Southampton was granted at the Principal Registry to William Humphrys of Montreux Bird Hurst Rise Gentleman the Father and Next of Kin.

HUMPHRYS William.
Personal Estate £1,560 4s. 6d.

16 April. The Will of William Humphrys late of Birmingham in the County of Warwick Fishmonger who died 22 January 1886 at 21 Belgrave-road Edgbaston Birmingham was proved at the Principal Registry by Harriet Ward Widow and Ambrose Philip Ward Fishmonger both of 21 Belgrave-road two of the Executors.

HÜNCKEN Ahrend.
Personal Estate £120 10s. 1d. in England.
Resworn December 1886 £1,770 10s. 1d.

22 July. Administration (with the Will and Codicil) of the Personal Estate of Ahrend Hüncken late of Hagen in Prussia who died 18 January 1886 at Hagen was granted at the Principal Registry under the usual Limitations to Adam William Burn of 13 Moorgate-street in the City of London Solicitor the lawful Attorney of Dorette Hüncken Widow the Relict the sole Executrix now residing at Hagen.

HUNDLEY Walter.
Personal Estate £654.

30 November. Administration of the Personal Estate of Walter Hundley late of 2 Surrey-villas Long-lane Finchley in the County of Middlesex who died 13 October 1886 at 2 Surrey-villas was granted at the Principal Registry to Elizabeth Ann Hundley of 2 Surrey-villas Widow the Relict.

HUNNINGS {The Reverend Henry.
Personal Estate £811 17s. 6d.
Resworn March 1887 £1,322 12s. 6d.

28 July. Administration of the Personal Estate of the Reverend Henry Hunnings late of 20 Carlton-road Fitzhugh in the County of Southampton Clerk who died 4 May 1886 at 20 Carlton-road was granted at Winchester to Margaret Ann Hunnings of 20 Carlton-road Widow the Relict.

HUNNS Susannah.
Personal Estate £41 18s. 4d.

12 January. Administration of the Personal Estate of Susannah Hunns (Wife of Matthew Hunns) late of Walsoken in the County of Norfolk who died 19 June 1884 at Walsoken was granted at Norwich to the said Matthew Hunns of 10 Marsh-walk Walsoken Yeoman.

HUNT Abraham.
Personal Estate £89 9s. 7d.

22 June. Administration of the Personal Estate of Abraham Hunt late of Poltimore in the County of Devon Farm Bailiff who died 7 February 1886 at Poltimore was granted at Exeter to Mary Ann Hunt of 23 East-John-street Newtown in the County of the City of Exeter Widow the Relict.

HUNT Adèle de Havilland.
Personal Estate £349 19s. 11d.

18 February. Administration (with the Will) of the Personal Estate of Adèle de Havilland Hunt (Wife of the Reverend Henry Warwick Hunt Clerk) late of Shermanbury Henfield in the County of Sussex who died 28 November

225

Fig. 34 Hunnings Estate details

Their daughter Madeline Anna Maria Wood-Taylor was born in the summer of 1888, but by December 1888 John Wood-Taylor was declared bankrupt (Fig. 35) and for several years the Wood-Taylor family lived at a variety of addresses around the Leeds area. However, they finally got a financial break in 1893 when John's father died and left him an annuity of £105 pa.

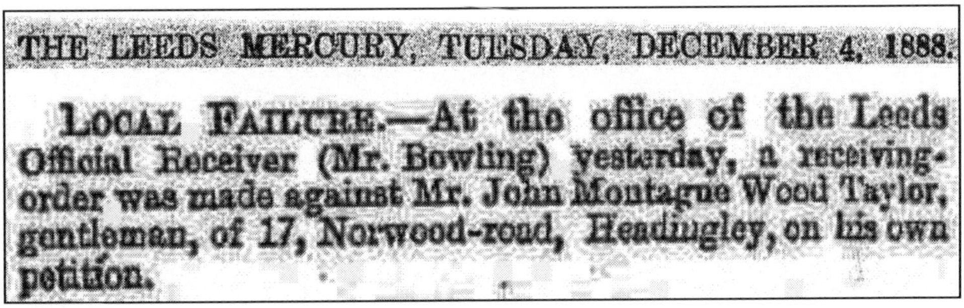

THE LEEDS MERCURY, TUESDAY, DECEMBER 4, 1888.

LOCAL FAILURE.—At the office of the Leeds Official Receiver (Mr. Bowling) yesterday, a receiving-order was made against Mr. John Montague Wood Taylor, gentleman, of 17, Norwood-road, Headingley, on his own petition.

Fig. 35 Leeds Mercury - Local Failure article

In 1901 they were still living in Leeds but shortly after moved to North Wales where they settled in Rhuddlan.

On 29th August 1912, at the age of 55, John Wood-Taylor died leaving Margaret a widow once again. Sadly, both her husbands having died at a relatively young age, and at the age of 51 she was on her own. She never re-married. John Wood-Taylor left only £72 5s 5d in his estate.

One might speculate that Margaret fell for the apparently eligible, well-to-do, gentleman John Montague Wood-Taylor thinking her future would be financially secure but it may be the case that John married Margaret for the same reasons.

All three children met and married their spouses in North Wales and went on to have children and families of their own. And then in order of their passing:

- Madeline Anna Maria died Q1 1937 age 48, in Chesterfield

- Margaret Ann died a widow in Q4 1940 age 79, at Rhuddlan

- Katherine Mary died Q3 1965 age 83, at Rhuddlan

- William Butters Jr died Q4 1972 age 92, at Holywell

Final Conclusion

Henry Hunnings was born in Tottenham on 25th July 1842 and died at the age of 43 in Southampton on 4th May 1886. The following is a summary of his most notable highlights and achievements:

- Henry Hunnings grew up on the High Road, Tottenham where he lived from birth and worked as a 'Letter Press Printer' until he reached the age of 25.
- By all accounts he was a quiet, studious, generally reserved man who, given the choice, preferred to be in the background. Despite his bashful nature he had strong ambitions to be someone and achieve something.
- He was an able Photographer and brought this emerging profession into the family business. His photograph of Hare Pomare now resides at the National Library of New Zealand.
- He was a family man. Regardless of the circumstances leading to the conception of his son William Butters (jr) he dutifully married Margaret Ann Ridley before the child was born and together in wedlock they had a second child Katherine Mary.
- He gained a BA and an MA at Oxford.
- His career in the Clergy whilst unremarkable was successful. From newspaper reports he was clearly an able exponent of his duties as Curate and Chaplain until his health deteriorated.
- He was an able pianist. Evidence exists through

newspaper reports that he played the harmonium and the organ on occasion at church services and events.

- The time Hunnings spent at Bolton Percy was undoubtedly his most significant but arguably ultimately lead to his demise.

- He passed on his knowledge and learning to others. From January 1882 to at least August 1884 he tutored schoolboys at his home, Portland House, Ryde, Isle of Wight. He delivered many lectures about the telephone and was called as an expert witness in court.

- He was a Conservative. He was elected to the Committee of the Ryde Conservative Group & was a regular public speaker in that forum particularly speaking out against the Liberals.

- There is evidence through newspaper reports that he was popular and well liked. Clearly he had a sense of humour too if the evening of the Eling Choral Society's closing entertainment of the year held on Thursday 30th April 1885 was anything to go by. There was a wide and varied programme that evening principally of piano solos and songs but there were *"two readings by the Rev H Hunnings, curate of Eling which were 'The Bashful Man' and 'A Night with a Stork'"*. I'd like to think this was a poke of fun at himself before an unknowing audience.

Undoubtedly, however, it will be for his work as an inventor, introducing the carbon-granule microphone to the world, for which he will be remembered. That great inventor of the 19th Century, Thomas Edison, was so impressed by Hunnings' device that, although he had defeated Hunnings in Court on a technicality, he bought the Hunnings transmitter patent preferring it to his own.

Hunnings was clearly an expert on the subject, giving many lectures on the 'Telephone, it's Construction and History'. He also exhibited and demonstrated his 'Micro-telephone' at events and exhibitions up and down the country and in October 1879 was awarded a Medal at the prestigious Yorkshire Fine Art & Industrial Exhibition.

However, perhaps ironically, a significant later development was the expiry of the Key Telephone Master Patents – which included the patents for Bell's Receiver (expired December 1890) and Edison's Transmitter (expired July 1891). Upon expiry the rights for these and others passed to the British Post Office meaning the patents were available for use by agreement without fear of litigation.

With the wonderful benefit of hindsight it does seem that the litigation between UTC Ltd and Harrison, Cox Walker & Co was unnecessary. Certainly Hunnings did not enjoy the fall-out and although he did make £1000 out of it, by all accounts the experience weighed heavily upon him.

The British Post Office went on to adopt Hunnings' carbon-granule transmitter as their transmitter of choice until it was phased out in the 1980s some one hundred years later. A small but hopefully familiar selection of some of the telephones that used this transmitter are included in Appendix B.

In conclusion, it is perhaps a sad thought that Henry Hunnings did not live to witness and appreciate the impact his invention would have on voice communications around the world nor see that the small wealth he received from UTC Ltd did not provide more security and comfort for his family. Indeed, had he not died in May 1886 he may well have lived to see a positive outcome in both cases and, no doubt, achieved his life's ambitions as his status would have endured.

Whatever caused him to take his own life on 4th May 1886 will never truly be known. The effects of ill-health, loss of job, loss of income, and stress of court cases were all considered and mentioned at the time as possible contributing factors. Of course, there was no mention of the scandal he had lived with for six years but had kept hidden from view but there is no doubt it was a tragic finale. Sadly, he died and was buried in relative obscurity.

But the historians of Tottenham have never forgotten Henry Hunnings nor indeed any of the Hunnings family who lived at 516 High Road. They have benefitted greatly from the photographs both he and his descendants have taken over the years. And in the village of Bolton Percy where Henry enjoyed his most successful time, he is fondly remembered too and commemorated in the Church of All Saints' for his service to the people of that parish from 1874 to 1880 and for his invention there which made such a contribution to the modern world.

Appendices

Appendix 1: A description of Hunnings' carbon-granule transmitter in his own words

The following description and image (Fig. A) is an extract from Hunnings' US Patent 246512 dated 30th August 1881:

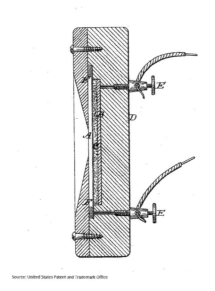

Source: United States Patent and Trademark Office

Fig. A US Patent Diagram

"It is shown embodied in a compact apparatus that can be freely handed about without liability to be injured. A front vibrating diaphragm, composed wholly or in part of suitable metal-such as platinum, silver, ferrotype-iron, tinned iron, and the like is employed. In close proximity to the aforesaid vibrating diaphragm is fixed a disk of brass or other suitable metal, and the intervening space is filled with carbon in the form of powder to the depth of, say, about one-sixteenth of an inch. The vibrating diaphragm and the fixed disk of brass are connected, respectively, with the opposite poles of a voltaic battery. The whole may be secured in a box of suitable non-conducting material, with a mouth-piece, if desired.

The way in which I prefer to carry my invention into effect is illustrated in the accompanying drawing, showing an enlarged section of the telephone-transmitter. The details can be indefinitely varied, the great feature being in the use of carbon in a state of fine loose powder, not in any way compressed or consolidated, as I find the loose particles of conducting matter to be most delicately sensitive to sonorous vibrations.

Referring to the drawing, **A** is the vibrating diaphragm, which I make very thin, preferably of platinum-foil, though thin ferrotype-iron, silver, or other metal, or a suitable metal-coated material may be used. It is held in place by the ring **F**, or in any suitable way, so as to permit it to vibrate freely.

B is the fixed disk or back plate, of brass or other suitable metal.

The intervening space between the diaphragm **A** and disk **B** is filled with the loose finely-divided conducting material **C**. I find the most advantageous result to proceed from the use of oven-made engine-coke, crushed very finely, not ground so as to pulverize (not to shear or tear) the particles, as I find the best results proceed from this. I may, however, use metallized carbon powder prepared with mercury or other suitable metal, if desired.

E and **E** are the binding-screws, placed in connection with the plates **A** and **B**.

The above is placed in circuit with a voltaic battery and receiving-telephone of suitable construction (such as Bell's) and the words or other sounds made close to the instrument, or otherwise, will be found to be distinctly and loudly reproduced at the receiving instrument.

The diaphragm, fixed disk or back plate, and case **D** might be altered in form, or be made oval or square, or other suitable shape, if desired; but the best results are produced if the instrument is made circular."

Appendix 2: Examples of some telephones which contained Hunnings' carbon-granule transmitter.

1. This first telephone, or what remains of one (Fig. T1), is an original Harrison, Cox Walker & Co Darlington manufactured telephone that would have included a Hunnings Micro-telephone and a Cox Walker receiver. Sadly, these have long since been lost. This example is from Beamish Transport Museum.

2. The second example (Fig. T2) dated approx. 1892 is an early Bell Telephone from the United States featuring a 'Hunnings-Cone' carbon-granule transmitter.

3. Then follows pictures of three early 'Bakelite' Post Office telephones. The earliest being the Tele 150 (Fig. T3) dated approx. 1920 and which was later modified to take a dial.

4. This telephone was succeeded by the Tele 232 series (Fig. T4) dated approx. 1930 and later the Tele 300 series (Fig. T5) which was first introduced before World War 2 and still in production in the 1950s. All three of these examples had Hunnings carbon-granule transmitters.

5. The first moulded plastic Post Office telephone was the ubiquitous Tele 706 (Fig. T6) first introduced in 1959. There was even a new carbon-granule transmitter manufactured for this phone in 1965. This was the Transmitter No. 16 (Fig. T7) which was the last production of a Hunnings transmitter by the Post Office.

Fig. T1

Fig. T2

Fig. T3

Fig. T4

Fig. T5

Fig. T6

Fig. T7

Fig. T8

6. Finally the Tele 746 (Fig. T8) which was manufactured from the late 1960s. The third generation of this telephone produced in the 1980s featured a replacement to the Hunnings carbon-granule transmitter.

Acknowledgements

The Author would like to give thanks to the following people and institutions who helped along the way, as the phrase goes these are in 'no particular order':

Helen Milton, Alan Swain (Tottenham Summerhill Road – no relation!), Beamish Transport Museum, BT Heritage & Archives, Bruce Castle Museum (Haringey Archive and Museum Service), St Edmund Hall University of Oxford, Wolverton Benefice, Cleveland Institution of Engineers, Friends of Southampton Old Cemetery, Tadcaster Library, British Library, London Metropolitan Archives, West Yorkshire Archive Service, to Martin Rice for giving me the idea and finally to my family and friends for helping and supporting me on this journey.

In addition the following reference books were consulted:

Memories of a half century (1899) – Richard William Hiley Vicar of Wighill

The English Adventurer – JG Bentinck